It Starts from the Belly and Blooms

poems

Thomas Fucaloro

THREE ROOMS PRESS

NEW YORK CITY

Some of these poems have been published by:
Keep This Bag Away From Children, Awosting Alchemy, Anatomy, Clutching at Straws, Free Verse, and others

First Edition

ISBN: 978-0-9895125-4-1

Library of Congress Control Number: 2013949714

Cover art:
"Wordsmith" © Kristopher Johnson (deeptanks.com)

Cover and interior design:
Kat Georges Design, New York, NY (katgeorges.com)

Text set in Adobe Caslon Pro

Published by Three Rooms Press, New York, NY
threeroomspress.com | facebook.com/threeroomspress

This book is dedicated to Demolisher.
Only he knows the truth.

contents

It Starts from the Belly
and Blooms

Waking up in a bathtub full of ice cubes

The heart is an organ best served cold.
I think she's the one. I know it.
She has to be. She sparkle ray light.
She has the kind of ass that can make you purr.
She kept making sure our drinks were full.
Her eyes sparkled moon June blossoms in mid May.
She is the one for me.
My Saturn runs rings around her Jupiter.

She   let   me   kiss   her   neck.

We went back to my place.

Immaculate love making sin shall begin.

As I kissed her left breast I started feeling
woozy, wired, wound and wobbly and way
underneath consciousness and fall.

Waking up in a bathtub full of ice cubes
I am numb but alive reminded of the womb.

Can't feel my body but try moving.

Something doesn't feel right.

My backside right side aches.

Feel a line of ridges and bumps and wire and stitches.

I had been opened up like a flower.

I gave her my heart

and she,

she took my kidney.

Waiting on line at Ralph's Ices

A father and his 5 year old boy are in front of me.

The boy picks up a plastic used dirty spoon
off the concrete and puts it in his mouth and his father
slaps it out of his hands and yells,

"Bad Michael. What the fuck are you doing? That's it, no ices."

Grabs his boy's arm and walks away.

If I were the father

I would have gotten a raspberry fudge ice for myself
and eaten it in front of the boy.

Raising a child seems difficult.

Lizards and video cameras

I'm the kind of fellow who enjoys the simple things
flowers, rainbows, butterflies and watching lizards
devour snakes on PBS.

When some idiot with a video camera and a low IQ
and a jacket vest is chasing and filming lizards
I'm a happy guy. TV and nature.

But then something happened,
it was like a new form of reality television.
They attached these miniature cameras
to the lizards' backs and let them loose
into the wild of controlled nature.

Lizards wearing video cameras.

At first I thought it was a union thing
ya know not enough people paying
their dues   send in the lizards.

Then I thought this berry vodka is berry good
because then I think I'm watching a Pixar film.

Then I think maybe the lizards are being used
to find underground terrorist cells which would
be like an awesome Pixar film.

Then I think I don't know what to think.

Then I don't know what to think turns into
I wonder what the lizard thinks....

The other lizards are gonna give me such shit about this.

Oh and that fucking scaly tailed prick Lenny
is gonna start talking about how I'm just a child's pet
and how he's dating my ex-wife and how he has

a fully ossified skeleton and I don't
and how I'm an alcoholic
and maybe it could be
a DreamWorks film.

This berry vodka *is* berry good
but then I get this dragging feeling
holding my body afloat.

What else is out there where we can attach objects to other living things?
Are there other possibilities?
What will help define in years to come?
What can we make of all this?

He walks to the edge of the George Washington Bridge and whispers Helen

Our bridges are what connect us.

Some stories have happy endings.
Some endings have happy stories.
Some stories sink like coral reef stones.

He whispers Helen
as if she could hear him
some other entity in a galaxy
far from his.

The souls of the lost in these
wondrous beams of steel
are a testament to those
who have chosen to jump.

He touches his chest
there's no pulse
but try telling that
to Helen.

Sammy the nerdy, depressed but optimistic poet-penguin-boy

They say my wings have evolved into flippers.
What's evolution without flight?

I am told because of my enormous girth
that girth don't get up off the ground
it just leaves you standing there, waddling.

What's black and white and red all over?
A penguin with a lot of heart.

Feeding on krill, fish and squid
is not a proper way
for a poet-penguin-boy to live.

I want to be able to hover over an almost dead carcass
waiting for that last calm of breath, that last pinch of light
so I can swoon on down buzzard hard
and eat what life remains.

What's black and white and red all over?
A penguin who reads too much Anne Carson.

I am an aquatic living force I am what can't,
will become, what shall be, I need a cliff
a mountain a starting point to prove my worth
to prove that believing in yourself is all you need.

Sammy the nerdy, depressed but optimistic poet-penguin-boy
walked to the edge of Frontier Mountain.

Felt the sun glisten his beak into a beacon
an open door into the righteousness of breath
he spread those flippers but in his mind
he only saw wings and he soared

for about 3 seconds

until he fell and kept falling and falling.

What's black and white and red all over?
A penguin who believes in himself.
A penguin who believes he can fly.

Animal of a different fang

Split your head right in two
like opening at the middle of an 800 page book
but each page does not fall into place
and there are words everywhere
even in your hair
so I took out my carving knife
pointed towards your destruction
but what rose was something much worse

8 more heads appeared
I had my katana blade
but only 7 fingers left
the other 3
sliced off
on some abandoned snow patch
at the foothills of the thunderous Crane Mountains
a large looming oak tree graces the white
with new born bark of fang.

Something races straight down it.

It's a squirrel.

It sniffs at my fallen left pinky.

He decides

it's not a nut.

The moon is a gentle reminder

Body pulls closer to insides
until backwards, dead and smiling
sets him out to sea.

Reborn burning hot the rising sun
but what about the lost oceans of the moon?
The swallow of ocean raises the only thing that can

a woman

swallows red the setting sun.

She bends back, arms up, still hungry
she swallows the light left by the sun
arms raise still hungry.

Apologies yearn the tongue.
Leave sterile for sorry and let body burn sky
until
red
until
swollen
until
wounds
clean
what we want to say.

Tell the sky everything
is going to be all right.

She runs her fingers through my hair.
I can't speak.
She has already cut my tongue out.
My words are lost on the open of the shoreline.
She continues to drag me to the ocean
my body bent around the words I'm sorry.
She cannot hear me.

The moon is a gentle reminder of every woman
who has drowned a man without apology.

Cheating on your lover on your wedding day

Was gonna eat Jesus' body but I knew they would have food at the reception

Being at this wedding I understand that I don't understand myself

My heart says *No* but the tapeworm in my intestines says *Love is beautiful*

And the pulse in my neck reminds me I'm alive.

Being at this wedding I understand that I don't understand myself

When I'm with insane people dancing it gives me perspective

The pulse in my necktie reminds me I'm almost dead

You're not as important as I need you to be.

When I'm with insane people dancing it gives me perspective

Hope is the biggest killer among folks

Your kiss is not as important as I need it to be.

I regret kissing your neck.

Hope is the biggest killer among folks

Love is a morphine drip

I regret kissing your neck

You say tomato I say post partum depression.

Love is a napkin

My heart has yet to crumble

I don't smell anything but blue

It was another fluorescent light fixture moon.

The hippo on the diving board

we all watch. Up down 4 legs tremble
it's fun to watch the dripping pool of fear
in another thing's eyes. Or is it what we
jump into that fears us? I drink some
lemonade. He still doesn't jump.
I walk to the next booth. It's a horse
threading a needle with its fake hand.

There's nothing worse than going to your sister's dance recital, sober

Twirl spin froth at the lips with cuteness

these Ritalin taking 8 year oiled girls
dressed in sparkly sequined bee outfits
dancing and spinning in circles to the song
I Wanna "Bee" Free by some shitty group
covering the Monkees

and it really bothers me because it's 10 dollars for one beer
in this ritzy dancey place and I didn't bring weed with me
so I just sat there
taking it all in.

Act after act
of dance after dance
of cuteness after cuteness
and I wanted to puke
but couldn't because
I did not want to pay
those prices for a beer.

Then finally the finale.
One of the dance instructor ladies gets up to the microphone,
"This is for the men and women overseas.
We got him we finally got him"
and then a remixed version of the song In The Navy starts playing
and that would make sense because all the girls are wearing sparkly
sequined Navy outfits

and everyone's dancing
and everyone's cheering
and everyone's happy

so I walked to the ritzy refreshment stand
gave the guy a twenty
and got two beers.

My dog knows all my poems

What has the word "yes" gotten anyone but pregnant?

So we had a dog instead.

After we said "no" to the pregnancy
you needed something alive
so you got us toy-fox-terrier named Demolisher.

Now you're gone due to poor snorting decisions on my part
and I've been stuck with this dog for the past 10 years.

This dog was supposed to be a way to fill in the space between us
but now the dog and I lie around watching the View, Oprah and PBS.

I don't feel anything for this dog anymore
yet I can't fall asleep without him.

I think she thought he would change me.

I wonder if I would have changed if we had the kid?

A 23 year old coke head buying baby formula.

Sounds like a great title for one of my poems.

I always think about that one moment that could have been
a small nubbed hand that I created wraps around my finger
just holding on.

I wonder does your spirit change or your sense of being or purpose
or is it all just a crock of shit?

There are days I feel lost without you and you aren't anything anymore.

Now I'm just sitting in my room
my dog asleep at my feet
listening to me recite this eulogy
just trying to hold on.

What has the word "no" ever gotten me but poems?

No use crying

Have you seen Carolyn Taylor?
Eyewitness news and the police are searching for her.
She was last seen walking home from school.
She is 8.
If you have any information please contact
Eyewitness news or the police.
We care for our children
brought to you by the Ford Motor Company.

Even missing children have sponsors now.

I used to think that missing children on the back of milk cartons
was just an advertising tool to sell more milk.

Milk doesn't need missing children to sell.

When I was younger I had no brothers or sisters
so that missing child on the milk carton became
a great sibling to talk to.

I remember cutting the missing child's head
from out of the milk carton and then the eyes
so I could see the world like them.

What I discovered was all children see the world the same

lost.

I also discovered that you need to drink the milk first before cutting the carton.

Growing Flowers—after Jeanann Verlee's Country Hard

My belly's as soft as the ocean.
Got a lighthouse. Shines its light on things worth eating.
It can't work a tractor. A blender. A dumbbell. A nautilus machine set
  on stun.

My belly's good with rum. It's a pirate. Vodka with everything makes
  good breakfast.
Women don't like a man whose belly can out drink hers it belches. They
  like a man conscious.
Awake. Women like a clean mouth. Some say it's over my belt buckle.
Some say they know it's over fat ass docker pants. Over other's bellies.
  Over and under.

My belly's got tape worms for teeth. An esophagus, an intestine and a
  hunger.
It taught animals how to be digested. Nurses the fat with some ice cream
  and a glass of Jim Beam. Falls flat on its ass when Jim Beam keeps
  touching. Don't mind that he still does.
It became its own man when size 34. Got its own census application.
  Got its own social security card. Got its own belly. Became a
  mountain. And nobody stand proud like my belly.
They say you can pull a rainbow out with your hands where the ocean
  begins and my mountain ends. Seen it ripple like ideas. Got itself a
  determination
stored up in the chest. Raised with momma's manicotti
under my tongue. Practiced weekends on raviolis.

My belly runs the digestive system without prejudice. All thoughts and
  ideas are eaten even if alive. Meat till it was 25, got an ocean full of
  other animals' body parts.
It would throw up now if it ever ate a big mac. Women like a clean mouth.
As long as it loves right and can eat a good vegetarian chili. My belly's
  proud flesh
is as warm as a baked apple pie.

Pillows your head softly
as your eyes meet mine. Women like a man with skills.
Took the life force it got, started teaching women how to be pregnant.

Ones with good family and hope in their genes.

It speaks about *how we should be in love first*. No child. Not yet.

Takes her to the clinic. Pays.

Talks about wounded dreams. Wounded wombs. Knows about being slippery.

About america. Curses the riot called morals. It smells of vinegar and
morning tears.

My belly's gotten sterile. Women like a man with a clean mouth. Like the sun
without the risk of light. My belly's got life. Got light. Got a way with
running away from it.

It's a mountain again. Some stretch of skin, poems deep.

Bury the hatchet.

In my belly.

Looking to make a clean mouth.

It speaks of growing fires and letting them go.

*(A Staten Island mother was arrested for burning
her 11 year old son with a red hot butter knife
to teach him a lesson.)*

The many uses of knives

Heated dull blade on stove top ready for scorching
a young boy picks his heart up from off the floor
and puts it back in his chest, unwashed.

The blade sizzles skin blistered off
ready to peel like colorforms

Hey mommy, look what's inside

I've got many various knives in here

like that cold carbon steeled machete
hanging from my ribcage that my father
left me when he left me for another addiction

or

there is that ever-changing titanium butterfly
knife with leather grip and upholstered age
of conceit that you would even think of touching
me this way

or

or my teeth are just various blades all in a row
these beaded blasted blade beasts lining my lips
are the cornerstones of how vicious my mouth
can truly be

or

the knives god gave me

my forearms embrace
my fist the handle my bone
white elbow the steel
ready for prey

or

these eyes
this sense of being
these blades of lashes
my knives are all matter being
my knives are all smatter bleeding
I am made of sharp and violent things

or

there's that small rusted dulled butter knife blade
you gave me,
more than once
dangling from my heart.

One day
it shall
enter yours

For you see
mother
my knives
they teach lessons too.

i before e except after vodka

Middle-aged-poet-boy has got to move back in with his mom.

Wounds heal all time.

What new ones shall we produce together?

Middle-aged-poet-boy only pays the bills when the collectors come
either them or the organ donor people.

Middle-aged-poet-boy drowns himself in Bukowski every night
and reads poems from the bottle.

Pour the notion of similes into a glass and burp out a poem.

Middle-aged-poet-boy does not try to pick up girls
because he is a middle aged poet boy.

If Thomas was a middle-aged-stock-broker-boy he would be hitting on girls
left and right of what the heart beats.

Middle-aged-poet-boy has stalks of corn growing from his ears
but The Norton Anthology doesn't publish long ass stalks of corn.

Middle-aged-poet-boy finds it difficult to urinate while thinking of poetry.

His penis likes to let out things one at a time.

Middle-aged-poet-boy finds it difficult to use proper grammar
because he keeps writing fucking poems all the time.

.He keeps putting his periods at the beginning of the sentence
so he will never end

a-e-i-o-u and sometimes wine.

Middle-aged-poet-boy will never get it right.

Middle-aged-poet-boy only wears lipstick when he is sober
so in other words middle-aged-poet-boy does not wear lipstick.

Maybe that's why middle-aged-poet-boy is moving back to his mom's house
because I never wear lipstick.

Dear Starbucks,

why would I drink your coffee
when I'm doing lines of coke in your bathroom?

Love, Thomas

If politicians aren't getting into
bar room brawls
then they aren't doing their jobs

It's amazing
how fair and balanced your decision making
becomes when hit by someone else's drunken fist.

If no one is taking a metal bat and a pint of ale
into congressional sessions then they aren't doing
their jobs.

I want my politicians sitting at the ends of bars
just watching the many find the few.

I want my politicians to do 72 hour keg stands
while discussing health care reform.

I want my politicians to spend time in a bottle
singing Jim Croce songs.

I want my politicians to be drunk on the human plight
and this motherfucker we call a country while sipping
cheap whisky.

I want my politicians to buy rounds of drinks
because it is their god given right to do so.

I want my politician's livers soaked in ether
and soft moments they might share with total strangers.

I want my politicians drunk like old men screaming
at their TVs.

I want my politicians unconscious and passed out
on
their mothers' couches.

I think when you are elected into public office
you should have to move back into your mother's house.

I think when you are elected to public office
you should listen to everything
your mother has to say.

Cocks

aren't for sucking

they're for running

for public office.

The new literature

They are looting in London but no one's touching the books.

They are looting in London and all they want are the

i-pods
espresso machines
dining ware
DVD players
designer clothing
earrings
TVs
disposable douches
but no one is touching the books.

They are racial profiling in London
because no one reads books anymore
they read instruction manuals for

pasta machines
video games
home entertainment centers
i-pads
cell phones
garlic mashers
paint ball guns

but books are the lost undiscovered islands of the ocean waiting for that open.

They are looting in London but no one is touching the books.
They aren't even reaching for them.

They're beating the fuck out of each other in London
because they are angry and emotional and irrational
just like the cops.

They are losing themselves in London
and the only place safe are the bookstores.

A book cannot stop a gun
but it can stop you from picking one up.

Violence is the new literature.

The new america

No one masturbates to books anymore.

They masturbate to

i-pads
video games
butt_fuck.com
tuber wear
digital erectile futures
and your brother's neighbor's wife's facebook photo.

but books are the lost undiscovered clitorises of the ocean waiting for that open.

No one masturbates to books anymore.

They aren't even fisting for them.

They're watching everyone fuck the fuck out of everyone on-line
because they are lost and insecure and horny
just like the cops.

They are losing themselves in their hands
and the only place quiet enough to masturbate
are the bookstores.

Masturbating cannot stop a gun
but it can stop you from picking one up.

A Typical Tuesday Night

I feel it go in.

I feel it go out.

Each thrust as grand and white chocolate truffled as the next.

She says, "Fuck me you beast," and I think of Kafka
and the thing I will need to become when this is all over.

I turn her over, her voice pounds my head.

Right before I'm about to cum
someone yells, "Cut, something is wrong
with the camera."

I take it out and put it away.

I walk back to my dressing room and finish myself off,
eat some cereal and stare out the window.

The moon seems like a pretty lonely place to be.

Staten Island brings out the death in me

It has dead fetus pockets everywhere sucking a little more of me in.

My inner chi grins
        because my inner chi is a spiteful son of a bitch
        longing the moment of breath dawned into blackened.

When will the raping of the mind begin
and I hope I get a good seat
because a good mind rape
is a gentle bird's silent song
dry fucking you over and under again
and all you can do is blush
like an old dirty dead
Cabbage Patch Doll
under the overpass
of Richmond Ave
and Authurkill Rd.

Even the death here
is fake.

If you claim to be an anarchist
then you are not a true anarchist
because titles and groups are
part of the social order

True anarchy

is eating nails

and shitting thorns

of crazed lunacy

lullabies cradle

the forehead.

You wear your vines on your sleeves.

They are veins of ivy

marionette style

you take your first step

towards becoming a growing shimmering bright yellow

sunflower.

True anarchy.

Valentine's Day is a great day for an ex-lover to get engaged

We lost a baby together

What did he ever do for you?

Diamond ring sparkle ray shine bursts
through my belly pulling out
stomach lining strand by strand
until there's enough to make a noose.

I go back to a time of dismal disarray
when we were puked, high,
worn and passed out lying
backwards of what our hearts beat.

I just want to be able to find you again
and grab you and let you know I'm special, I'm special too, don't you
    remember, I am, please
                believe me, I am special, I'm someone, I think

in tomorrow's light

I wish you nothing
but children and roses

but tonight, tonight is for the madness
and it dances on window ledges like
drunk 8 year old ballerinas
and you can't forget the past, no you can't
and I don't think you have
maybe that's why you were able to move on.

O' but I feel that fucking thing in me growing
every day but I never gain weight and never deliver
and it cries every night and I try and stop it
with nursery rhymes and gin and some nights
it talks back to me but always mundane conversation

"How are you doing?"
"I'm fine how are you."
"I'm ok but it's dark"
I never know what to say after that.
O' this longing weights eternal.
I feel something whisper in my ear.

Why   isn't it   someone?

No savings, no job

I'm 36 and have nothing.

I thought I was going to be dead at 33.

So at 36 not having nothing is really having something.

Life is a circle to the squares and the squares of the squares

or

Circling life with a crayon doesn't provide much color in-between the lines

or

Sons who get their fathers accidentally killed shall one day rise like the sun

or

The movie the Lion King is about a bunch of hippies who get way too high and think they are lions

We should all be baptized
with the juice of sacred
guava melons setting our
foreheads to the sands of
time, grinning.

Parents are proud of their born.

They have a whole lifetime to lose that.

Lion families seem happier than human families.

The sun sets with the passed
the shadow land just might be the future.

I laugh in the face of danger and danger is a pack
of flesh eating rotten breath breathing hyenas
that sound like Whoopi Goldberg and Cheech Marin.

Deliberately disobeying your father outcasts the heart.

We all have big paws to fill.

Looking for trouble is like looking for the sky
vast, surrounding and everywhere.

Killing Simba should be easy.

We all have a small roar.

Killing Simba has been as easy as trying to drink water out of a water buffalo.

Killing Simba should be as easy as killing the Lion King.

Some paws are worth filling.

Some Simbas are worth saving.

We all long for that roar.

Some Simbas are worth saving.

Blink and you can almost miss it
as the Lion King's brother, the evil Scar,
lets him fall to his death.

Killing brothers is part of the american dream.

Changing your past is like changing your socks
you're always going to have to change your socks.

I would break out into song but who's got time
with all this death going on.

We all long for that roar.

Some fathers die and some become the crisp Autumn air around us.
Some fathers are worth saving.
Some cubs are worth having.
Some green eyed glowing hyenas are worth killing.
Some animated lions are worth watching each other fight in slow motion.

We all long for that roar.

50 green eyed glowing hyenas is an awful way to die.
Ask a hippo about that.

Life is a circle.
Ask the sunrise about that.

We all have a small roar
it starts from the belly and blooms
like all true movements do.

There will be snow

Bed bugs in the Santa suits and reindeer droppings
in the eggnog. This is what Santa's off time is like.
He becomes fatter and dirtier. Starts cursing
out Mrs. Claus. Santa starts going
to a monthly group for anger management.
He eats all their cookies.

She wouldn't let me into her pants but she let me into her heart

To my upside down light bulb shaped girl
the only thing I understand is your lips.
They part a most eternal sunrise.
The open morning motion of hands clasp
what time is always ticking about.

To my upside down light bulb shaped girl
we in trance a soft silent hum of breath
mounting
we collide like children and glass doors.
You bring out this sap in me
that trees don't understand
yet embrace.

Leaves never forget.
They just fall.

My upside down light bulb shaped girl
I'd kill plants for you, smash a daisy,
stomp a patch of sunflowers
set fire to some roses
incinerate some petunias
whatever flower you want
dead shall die for our flower
shall sing anew.

Your hips shorelines amongst the waves
crash a most enchanted moon.

Our mushiness stands for no one but ourselves.

My upside down light bulb shaped girl
you're a devil dressed in angel skin
and peel the right amount of dark
to reveal the right amount of light
and I inhale your back
exhales of the soul waking.

I'm not looking to marry you
I just want to hold your hand.
You were sculpted by e.e. cummings pen
and you're just as confusing and just as radiant.
There's nothing better than kissing someone who believes in you.

Knows no choreography

It creeps upon me
drenched in pink.

Sits next to me on the couch
drinks some of my soda
eats some of my pop corn
we make out.

It gets up and goes
into the next room.

I can feel small bits
of kernel from its kiss.

Death knows no choreography
but still wears ballet shoes.

wilting flowers always dance in the moonlight
to the beat of each other's poetry
(for Brant Lyon)

So I remember this one night Bob Hart
featured at Otto's Shrunken Head
and he tore the roof off the place.

Anyone who was there had their poetic talents heightened.

Bob Hart showed us the way and we walk it every day.

He told us he had written it just for that feature
and threw the poem away. It was only for one use
like life
like this body.

Brant recovered it from the trash.
He had discussed turning it into a little Bob Hart chapbook.

Either way Brant understood the beauty of true art
and he always wanted to share in that by sharing just that.

I loved taking word baths in Brant's myriad
of phrases that opened parameters around doors
that never understood the word, *closed*.

Something about his way of thinking
will always remain close to the heart
by filling the veins
with ideas
turning them into poems

that matter.

So it looks like no more Brant word baths
in my immediate future
but there is this body
that I consume
only to be used once
like life
like wilting flowers dancing in the moonlight
like a Bob Hart poem.

Children double dutch in the endless moonlight
the zombies come, eat all their brains
it's a full moon tonight

They say hiding is the hardest part
but it's hard hiding from what you don't
understand.

We all are afraid of the undead.

Haunting pasts are like growing neck goiters
always in the way
always in plain sight.

Locked doors are an opportunity for death
but sometimes the unlocked ones come to the same conclusion.

I've never had a problem

running away

from my problems.

Having your brain eaten is like a 7 minute Tom Waits song
always crisp
always cool
always street lit just right.

When the zombies catch me
they won't find a thing
just a couple of buffalo headed nickels

a tender alto sax melody

a diamond

ring.

I want to go to a graveyard and take molly

He wants to go to a graveyard and drink beer.
We compromise. We do both. We use
the tombstones like backs of chairs.
He says his father is buried here.
We're all buried here one way or another;
I say that in my head. I know he didn't hear me
but I know he understands. He starts digging
for the heart I told him I buried here. I start
looking for the bones of his dead father
to build a fire.

I want to have children so that they can one day grow up
and watch me die

The hallway banister reminds me of my grandfather.

Each step as grand as the next
hard thump and strained
the metal banister would
squeak his song.

I didn't see him pass away
but I can see it a little in my mother
with every blink-lash-clasp oysters,
2 pearls rise and fall like 2 sunsets

My mother's body shape is changing like an opened hand, closing.

My mom made me get rid of my Transformers.

She never was comfortable with anything that changes.

My mom told me
the first night I moved back home

"I missed you and I'm a little nervous and I need you to be here to hold my
    hand when I die."

Her body is starting to give up on her.

Her mind is telling her it's over
and her heart beats this every 2-beat.

Will I be there when my mother dies

or will it be something

that I only see

in me?

– is a part of –

i think i'm going to die tonight.

i just got this chill.

it came up from behind me.

i could sense its shadow.

if i do not die tonight then i could just be overtired, hallucinations perhaps…?

but if i'm right

if i'm dead

you'll know there's something out there

that lets you know

you are gonna die.

The killing of Optimus Prime was a business decision

How do you transform death into life?

The answer
marketing.

I was 8 years old when the original Transformers the Movie came out
and death was a doorknob I had yet to turn.

When his eyes dimmed
      head turned
            faded a charred grey
                      no hope, no hope at all.

I was a suburban boy living in the suburban shit hole of Staten Island
and the Death of Optimus Prime is still with me.

He was the leader I always wanted to be.

So when I heard Optimus was killed off
because you wanted to add new characters
to increase sales I understood.

Killing heroes and profiting from it is part of the american dream.

Silly cartoon characters rock the night to sleep dreamin' of better
    mornings.

When you're 8 they are all you have.

Now at 36 most of my heroes are dead
or living in death smeared with cracked
concrete of desperation.

Optimus Prime isn't the poet Charles Bukowski was
but they both had a little blue bird inside of them.

The pen seeped in ink from the hand understands
that 8 year olds and profit margins are the same thing.

Even to a 35 year old the margin is a horizon I cannot find.

Guns don't kill people.

Cyber troopers from Cybertron with napalm guns do

and so do accountants.

They let you know who is expendable and who ain't.

Optimus Prime was expendable.
8 year old boys were expendable.
36 year old boys were expendable.

It was like a mob hit.

They gut the throat slowly but surely the wound speaks.

It drips out notions of long ago and how long ago is so present now.

Optimus Prime is not human.

But I am.

Ever the more reason to be concerned.

You have autumn in your eyes

I like the color of you.

We sip from each other like the gods do

big gulps

my chin hair damp with night drenched
in luscious lambs to slaughter one after one
you cum

and we rip the night to shreds
I mean we actually produced the sun
and it is only 9pm
the night never stood a chance against us.

I want to write a poem

on the back of your neck

with my tongue.

If you don't let anyone in then you can't let anything out

I like that you like to be naked.

We all like to be naked
except the trees.

No bark
no bite.

My body is a swan floating in acceptance
and my blubber doesn't understand ugly
and ugly doesn't understand us
that's why ugly
is ugly.

Wrinkled bodies mushing together are sometimes the prettiest of rainbows.

Boys don't cry but men do
over their bodies like anorexics
but hold it in and reflect it off
the person they're with as if
their bodies were placed here
in sacrifice for the failings of ours.

Sometimes smiles are difficult.

But so is math

and so is love.

Love is a pain in the ass but great to have dinner with.

I want to love my body but my soul won't so my mind expects you to be perfect.

I pretend to be desire but come out soft like cotton balls.

It takes time and understanding and alcohol
to accept who you are.

Life has got its ups and downs
like the missionary position
and I think you are really neat
and I feel we could eat, read and flower together
and stem well branch the trees to grow tall and proud
and what comes out of me into you is tall and proud
and nectar proves time and moan again that our bodies
are beautiful
especially when our bodies are beauti-fulling each other.

So I guess what I'm trying to say is yes,

I would love to see you naked too.

Garbage Day

Death is in bags around my feet.

Another grandparent passes away.
The stale moldy smell of life
once inhabited this place. I breathe—

We put what is left of them
in garbage bags and boxes
and bring them out to the curb.

It still smells.

i smile

knowing you
are without me
holding someone else
and i take my time with my neck tie
and i take my time with that thought

The day my mom made me
put my childhood into a box
and give it to Jared Singer

There is no one I would rather give my childhood to.

Bearded poets with fixable hearts
are what my childhood needs.

At some point parents become immune to toys
and their steadying of the heart.

I have put my Megatron gun to my temple many a night.

Hasbro gave me the characters
but I created the stories.

It was up to me to show character.

Some childhood stories
about action figures
are just dribble yet shape
what the mind hasn't thought of yet.

The things we don't see are most important.

That cycle of creating stories still rears
its ugly head into my head.

As a child I had Transformers everywhere.
As a quasi-post-pubescent-adult I have poems everywhere and
I don't give a shit if she makes me throw away those things too
but I wouldn't give them to anyone.

I would bury my poems like an old dead dog.

And they would rise
like the glistening morning sun
being eaten
and destroyed
by a planet
who eats and destroys other planets

Unicron.

class

There is a new yogurt shop that opened up
on the corner of Canal and Anal. Everyone
who came in requested fried chicken.

The yogurt people didn't know what to do
so they closed down and then a month later
reopened as a yogurt and fried chicken shop.

Everyone who came in asked if this place
had any class? The shop eventually shut down.
The answer to that question is yes, it did.

Using colors as numbers
or
Using numbers as children
or
It's not educational until someone's bleeding

When you think of blood you think of the color red.

Red or E122 reveals so many different feelings inside us.
For me I see anger and love or burnt sun rises or stripes
or carbon-hydrogen-nitrogen-sodium-oxygen-sulfur.

You see if you mix these elements together
and follow the directions with the proper
tablespoon usage you can create the color red
or as they say around the lab Allura Red AC
or FD & C Red No. 40 and these color and
sweeten our skittled-m&m-nerd-pops
and help to create something called

ADHD

or

Attention Deficit Hyperactivity Disorder.

Artificial coloring is part of the american dream.

Attention
Deficit
Hyperactivity
Disorder.

Took 3 tries before I wrote down the proper order of words for that condition.

Lately we've been blaming teachers and lawmakers and families for our
    children
not getting the education they deserve.

Blaming teachers for poor education is part of the american dream

but no one's blaming
E127, Erythrosine
or pink shades
or Blue No. 2 Lake
or coal tar
or jelly beans
or tartrazine
which can also cause depression
and when you are a child religion is candy.

Why isn't anyone saying maybe my child has some crazy
chemical shit inside of them that they shouldn't
and candy coatings don't always mean grandness,
they mean an imbalance of body chemistry and at a time
when their bodies are just learning how to balance.

It's what alcohol isn't at that age

and all this habdashery blaming unions and teachers and families for poor education
it's the Nerds, it's the Skittles, it's the Starburst-Big League Chew-Mike and Ike-
Bubblicious-Jaw Breaker-Lemonhead-M&M-mentality,

it's the candy

it's the red dye

number-1.

Touching

My middle school history teacher
told me dating students is a no, no, no.
but dating teachers is a yes, yes.

He rubs his hand over my thigh.

The police came
but only to watch.

Felt more like a release

My roommate has been ordering prostitutes
from Craigslist and he has a girlfriend.

How do you confront someone about this?

This isn't like normal roommate complaint stuff like
why don't you take out the trash?
why don't you buy toilet paper?
why are you peeing in the kitchen sink?

This gives me such an icky feeling
like when having too much sun
hit your face while drinking
warm milk.

I start thinking about diseases and wonder why
my roommate does not do the same?

Ordering prostitutes from Craigslist is part of the american dream.

I'm an open dreamer
who supports making love
or banging anyone you want
as long as it's consensual
and as long as there is
basking in the glistening sweat
of good morning's embrace.

Making love should be our chief export.

One night I got a Caesar salad with grilled chicken.
My roommate said, "I thought you were a vegetarian?"
"I've been eating meat every now and then."
He replied, "Cheater."

"Well at least I'm not cheating on my girlfriend
with prostitutes."

The punch felt more like a release and his fist
went right into my gut moving all my organs and goop
to the other side of my stomach.

He realized what he did and started apologizing
and started taking out the garbage and buying toilet paper
and he stopped peeing in the kitchen sink.

My roommate still lives with me
and he still orders prostitutes
and I still get grilled chicken
on my salad from time to time.

Facebook is a graveyard of lost lovers

In the morbid times of earth's embrace
the ground is wet yet sultry beneath my feet
and the trees' veins root down into the river
of miseries, long forgotten, reintroduced
to miseries already present in poems
by Lord Byron and the heart.

I never realized how sad and depressing facebook is.

All these statuses of lost love and the love they have found.

From friend to lover to facebook friend
I sit here alone in my room staring
at the epitaphs on my screen screaming
some other sunrise for someone else's
arms.

Facebook lets you know

how well they are doing

without you.

You get to watch them change into somebody else
right before your eyes and you get to comment
on that change as well....

Oh and comment I do....

for you see I am an immature 36 year old poet boy from Staten Island
so facebook allows me to be real petty and childish by leaving
such grandiose comments—

like on Erica's status I put

I hope the panties I got you are making someone else very happy or what I posted on Tania's wall

Sometimes you have to use someone to get over someone so you can love somebody else

or here's something I posted on Jacqueline's wall

While getting a blowjob I realized I miss you

O' facebook surely is a graveyard of dead lovers and lost dreams
and I certainly am one
of the Shepherds the grave diggers
the funeral fire
the burning torch
surrounded
by the black of night.

Some gravestones
they write themselves.

I don't need facebook
to tell me I'm dead
I'm a poet
I died a long time ago.

The worst thing we can do

is procreate

at a time like this

The sign said
Have a baby. Participate
in the new research lab.

So here

have a baby

and yes you yes over here

have a baby

and I didn't forget about you reading this

have a baby

I'm having one write now

hold on,

yes!

have a baby

so that they have some more babies
and then they have some more babies
and that's like 12 babies for the price of
sex

so here

have a baby

participate in the new research lab.

Oh wait
I've been reading the sign wrong
It's not *Have a baby*
as a statement.

It's *Have a baby?*
as a question.

Have a Baby?
Participate in the new research lab.

I saw this sign flashing on one of those flashing boards
at the entrance of a college and what this implies to me
is this college is asking if they can have students do tests
on your babies because it's a tax write off for corporations
and sometimes
you just don't have enough
mice
or men.

I don't know what this sign means
and I'm afraid to ask.

There is a whole culture out there testing the human condition
by conditioning the human out of you by prosthetic hair pieces
and bible belts all don't mind a little whatever
as long as that whatever
has a pulse
that needs a little something more
because nature is wrong
and Lysol is right.

It seems these days
they only test poisons
on children
at a college level.

How an 8th Grade Geography Student becomes a Man

The sexiest thing about you is what I learn.
Learning has such great curves.
The center of gravity spins it.
Land mass hips and long splendorous kisses hum it.

Learning has such voluptuous curves.
The roots of the trees can feel it.
Land mass hips and long splendorous hiss hum of breath.
This pinnacle pour of undiscovered youth silks the tongue into ravenous
    delight.

The roots of my tree start to feel it.
I am a great nation under control of body.
This pinnacle pour of undiscovered youth silks my heart into puberty.
I am a land mass unto myself strong and mighty.

I am a great nation under control of body.
Oh and the center of gravity spins it
like a simple classroom geography globe
set on fire.

Your lips.

It's hard to tell the students from the madmen

Part 1

We are 70% water and 30% fucked up.

It's that fucked up-ness that dictates who you are.

It's a crown of writ prone
to be sewn to the head
like a cabbage of hair.

The ocean inside all of us is only as useful as who we let drown in it.

The sun is always shining much brighter in my head.
I see with my looks and mind with my eyes.

The often heartbeat cellos a bow across the wrinkles of your forehead
to a tune only found in mental patients on heavy medication
dripping drool
the only words that pour from their mouths.

In Staten Island once stood the Willowbrook Mental Institution.

Regenerating impulses of normalcy
into a pulse migrating to its own hum.

Medicated intravenous introverts roaming
the halls of this once proud institution

laughing
    all the way
            to the other side of the room.

Now the Willowbrook Mental Institution has been torn down
and out from its ashes now stands the College of Staten Island.

Regenerating pulses of normalcy
into an impulse to migrate into itself.

Medicated post-adolescent introverts roaming
the halls of this now proud institution

learning
    all the way
            to the window.

Pills inspire as well as medicate.

Books inspire as well as medicate.

Learning institutions are the new mental hospitals.

We are 30% water and 70% fucked up

and 100% everywhere.

Part II

Every day is a reason
to get fucked up.

I was waiting for the #59 bus to go to the College of Staten Island.
The Seaview Mental Hospital bus stopped instead.
It wasn't my bus but you can understand why it would want to stop for me.
It's hard to tell the poets from the madmen.

When a wrist can produce pen produce light
they always want to put you away
just in case
you are its source.

*(From the point of view of a 64 pack of crayola crayons
in your hall closet behind the board games as the spirit
of Walt Whitman moves from color to color)*

Why won't you hold me anymore?

Why won't you melt me in bottle caps
and show you what a real color can do
from solid to lava without losing the hue
of wonder a color can change

it can perceive time by giving it dimension

and those dimensions outside the lines a rainbow does one make.

But that is when I was sea green with optimism

but the only color colored dark

this closet

door never opens

and whatever wonder a child loses becomes a spirit
blends white with silver with copper with sky blue
with some tangerine and every day one crayon color
comes alive but often hands lose

touch

knows now

of opportunity

and opportunity doesn't have a color

just a hunger.

Oil canvas paintings of New Jersey
with all these bears wearing
hunting gear shooting
all these humans
floating in my head

When bears find themselves
in the backyard of some suburban
family they are labeled a terror
or an intruder or a killer.

Thank god
nothing happened
to the children.

When humans go into the forest
and start hunting bears
they call that american.

Thank bears
nothing happened
to New Jersey.

For one week of the year New Jersey residents
are allowed to go hunting for bears.

They should make a law where residents
can go hunting in the governor's mansion
for allowing such a stoopid form of brutality.

Hunting bears is a part of the american dream.

On the news they showed an 11 year old boy
who shot this massive mother black bear.

Children should not be killing mothers no matter what species they are.

I really have been taking an interest in the art of the human tragedy.

When I see someone in a cast I say good
serves them right the karma that spins
round and hits total strangers upside the head.

Crutches are just chopsticks for the gods to slurp you up with.

I'm starting to take comfort in the warm spring blanket called human suffering.

I just don't feel bad anymore.

I'm just numb.

Lose an arm here lose a limb there I just don't fucking care anymore.

Don't worry we still have actors who can play you in movies to know you are alive.

I have officially become cleansed and set free and numb to violence.

When you see a news story
of an 11 year old boy who killed
a mother black bear
in New Jersey
because it was legal
you think what I was thinking—

it sounds like a Thomas Fucaloro poem

but it isn't
it's out there
in New Jersey
showing our children how to create true art
with true death
by just a stroke of the brush
and a bullet to the head.

The Three Headed Monster Squid Things

The world seems like a scary place when you are not fucked up.

The rain for some reason doesn't taste as good.

I've noticed the trees more and the dirt and the news.

I understand that the world don't understand
the tremors in someone's hand and how a soft slow hum
of pills assures safety in numbers and smiles.

I feel lately like a one armed poet.
Like something's missing. Like my stump wants
to branch out my fist flourishes a moonbeam
of wants and haves but can't seem to get around why
my fist won't open without a pill.

Soberism is playing with my head.
I can smell the grass now but I don't dare step on it.
I dare not travel without a pill in my throat and a lump in my kidney.

I can't stop saying pills in my poems and they can't stop taking 'em down.

Why does all this beauty around the world not encompass me
into its savory clutches?

My life lines tread like stock market tickers
and I seem to now have inherited a mass amount
of someone else's debt and I need a drink
or possibly 3 drinks and a vicodin.

When I was fucked up on coke
I used to see Republicans, Democrats and Liberals
running around but now with soberism in place
3 headed monster squid things is all I see.

Drugs help remind me we are all human.
Sometimes revelations are more important than revolutions.
Should street criminals control drugs or should the business criminals?
I tend to go for street criminals because they seem more honest.

And this is why soberism is bothering me because then I'm left sober
focused. Trying to decide where I belong among the street criminals
or the business criminals or the 3 headed monster squid things.

I can now see all this ugliness in the world.

It used to be
when I was fucked up
the only thing that was ugly
was me.

Air in a Frame

Part I

Hooked up to machines the heart beats.

Peel skin and you will only find more skin.

Brittle bone bark keeps going BEEP BEEP BEEP.

Alabaster rose glow thoughts revive us of better days
and better beeps but often time holds moments in a
frame with nothing but breath.

What does one say in these matters
especially when the other person's brain
can no longer recognize your voice?

The old man in the bed next to you
beeps a different song
but the chorus is quite the same
and the only breath left to frame
is in your left breast pocket
next to your pen and scraps of paper.

Part II

I'm in some sort of financial straits.

I'm 34, living with my mom and broke.

When I heard you had a cardiac-arrest
a part of me felt this relief
I knew you left me a little something
in your will.

My relief turned into bewilderment.

What kind of person am I, relieved with
some sort of money compensation because
of your death and what kind of society
would allow for this emotion to birth?

We are at the point in our economy
where dead relatives = a good income.

Hair Appointment

Each box resembles the next. One long rectangle.

How can the last week in February become the first week in March?

I haven't forgotten responsibility only time.

Whether it becomes March or dementia as long as something begins.

My son says he'll let me know when it is my time to go.

I will tell you when it is my time to go.

I am an offering, a box, a long rectangle.

Good evening ladies and gentlemen my name is Thomas Fucaloro and I am a vessel

(when the gods start talking through me)

The clouds part a way into eternal happiness.

Eternal happiness has height restrictions as to moral judgment.

The earth moves in slow movements
to revitalize the large steps you might
take to find us.

We spin it in order for light to capture eyes
of disillusionment.

The sun barely knows you exist anymore
but we do and shine shall ominous sky squints
at the force of your light.

If you never find us

don't worry

we shall still wait for you.

(the preachers, they start talking through me)

Oh I gotsta tell you Jesus is my Audi Dealer
and I'm ready to drive to thy savior he will be
hitchhiking oh and I am ready to pick him up
and receive him

because God needs saving

in each resound shutters an echo of intangible
bone breaking into bits and I gotsta tell you
when these bits bind together they scream
god and how god can god be screaming in eternal

glory as damnation need not whisper a thought
into ear.

Oh I can see you right through the TV screen
it is as hot as a virgin mother up in here
a shimmering moon dove light is your past
it's a present to be unwrapped and today
is your birthday so look back on yesterday
as a gift and today as a moral choice
let light in.

(then Thomas Fucaloro starts talking through me)

I don't believe in god
but I do believe in the healing power
of people who do.

We shall never reach him.

We can barely reach the moon.

God doesn't need saving.

All god needs is a good woman.

Someone to rub his shoulders and talk about the ever expanding universe with.

A woman is an ever expanding universe.

God knows this.

and that's why I think we don't need him

we just need women.

I can't believe I let you touch my balls

Most people don't know this about me

but I am an 18th century-dainty-antique-delicate-cracked-Japanese tea cup.

When the Japanese mend a broken object
they aggrandize the damage by filling it
with gold. When something has suffered
damage it becomes more beautiful.

She said she knew who I was.

She said she was afraid of my past
little did she know
so was I.

Oh haunting pasts are like growing neck goiters
always in the way, always in plain sight
and she didn't have a problem reminding me

of the 10 year cocaine habit thing
the unemployed thing
the poet thing
the you've only been sober from coke 2 years thing

and rehabilitation doesn't always mean promise
and she thought me not a gentleman to keep.

She claimed my petals had long fallen off
but little did she know
that bud blooming in the wind
is a rising sun

and I have crawled out of shit and seizures and
I ain't ever going back to up my nose so fuck you
it is me who is saying my light is way too bright
for you

I was the dry spell and then the storm

thieving, lying, deceiving, deceptive,
dreadful, dirty little rocks snorted through brain
I am the fire of ash the burnt over with heart
I resurrect thee and your judgment of me
is just another candle lit on this journey.

I am the journey
you were nothing but a path.

It's never too late to be yourself.
If someone ever says to you you can't
show them the well lit back alleys of your torso
this city breathes for change and yearnful light

2 years ago I used to have to say,
"Hello, my name is Thomas Fucaloro and I am addicted to cocaine"
now I say
"Hello, my name is Thomas Fucaloro and I am a New School MFA Creative
    Writing student"

and you know who was there for me, I was there for me
if anyone says it's too late tell them it's too early to jump from bridges
and you know what they say cocaine abuse does lead to literary MFA degrees
and you can keep cutting my limbs but like a starfish I keep regenerating back

so yes I am a motherfucking-super-bad ass
-18th century-dainty-antique-delicate-cracked-Japanese tea cup

I am damaged but I am beautiful.

My mouth is a well
you can certainly
put your wishes here.

That shit

Leaving a lover

in heat

is like leaving a $100 bill on the sidewalk.

Someone else is gonna pick that shit up.

Some look at the glass as half full
some look at the glass as half empty
I look at it like a six pack

or

A beautiful wound

or

I drink responsibly; it is my responsibility to drink

or

I don't think I should drink anymore

yet

I think I should drink more

Where does the art end and the soberness begin?

Some look at the glass as half full
but I see it as broken on the street by the curb
with rats rummaging through it like a last day bake sale.

Can't seem to find the write rhythm in my heart
so I try to drown it making it become a raft
with a little penguin on it waving, hi.

The soft-little-sweet-cuddly-cute-evil-crazed-fucking-penguin-thing
inside of me is an enabler with its cute and its warmth
and its degenerating need to want a PBR with a shot of Jack
on the side every 13 heartbeats.

The soft-little-sweet-cuddly-cute-evil-crazed-fucking-penguin-thing
keeps convincing my poems they need more whisky.

The stubble around my face seems concerned.

All work and no play makes Jack a dull boy.
All Thomas and no Jack makes my poems a dull boy.

My poems are addicted to alcohol.
I'm addicted to poems.

And the soft-little-sweet-cuddly-cute-evil-crazed-fucking-penguin
is addicted to the lunacy of it all making me mad dog fodder
to throw to the wolves when the sun is not looking.

My poems have become luscious mad dog fodder
the wolves can smell it
on their poems.

It's a lonely chilly night in Manhattan
but the beat is just right
dripping wet petals
on sidewalk pavement crack
a couple of needle points of grass
find their way out.

There's hope in that one tiny crack
that we misname *things the city needs to fix.*

The more cracks in the sidewalk
the more the earth is trying to open itself up
like a flower
like a fist
like a car trunk
like a bottle of Heineken
like a jar of paint
like a womb
like a beautiful wound

crying concrete crying *Fucaloro!*

I raise my arms in the air and scream

I AM LUSCIOUS MAD DOG FODDER!"

Which one of you wolves is gonna save me?

What Tom and Jerry said behind the scenes

"You never loved me.
Always the meat you're after
never the wonder the why
an embrace.

"I always wanted to hold you
but the cameras were always
rolling.
I turned that negativity towards you.
I'm sorry."

"Oh you know you like the thrill of the chase
the almost
got

you

but falling short
of an embrace."

"If an embrace is all it took
then let the fires burn wild
because thou art the burn."

"This is just you chasing me again, isn't it?"

"No it's not."

"Yes it is."

"No it's not."

"Yes it is."

"Ok, maybe just a little."

"Yeah I thought so."

"Well what can I tell you?"

"You can tell me you won't chase me again."

"I can't. I'm a cat."

"Oh, yeah well I'm a catch
and you could have all this
if you just took the time
to get to know me."

"We rain just so we know we can fall.

My hope blood deep
for you. My clawed blood instincts
bury for you. My gray hair shouts waves
for you. My ocean parts days for you. I wish you nothing
but a paw, a sorrowing hunger
that has been stifled by every hole
in the wall in this moment we should
touch

without big red hammers
without MGM's consent
without dynamite
without commercials
without fire."

Jerry closes his eyes.

His pulse racing like a squirrel high on speed.

"Let me always feel you even after I am gone."

Tom grabs Jerry.
Throws him down his gullet and waits.
Inhales, exhales
3 times
swallows.

In the gallows of his neck down
in an ocean of water colored dreams
control this cartoon canopy controlled
by intestines outlined in ink.

Tom rubs his belly twice
curls up
alone.

Jerry dissolves away
becomes a passing memory
a ghost
lighting this stage
this book, this pedestal
this moment
and you
were the only ones
who saw it.

Cancer is so romantic

We have learned to live with it
sleep with it
put it on its back and make love to it.

I can't put my finger on it
but cancer feels more
like a commodity now.

This corporation will cause the cancer

and then this corporation will cure it

over

a long

period

of excruciating

time.

I tried to take out a loan at the bank.
They said, "No, but would you like some cancer instead?"
Whatever happened to toasters?
Cancer is now a part of the culture.
What ever happened to pop songs?

I would do you if the lighting was right

When you let me touch your breasts

I started liking your poems.

We are all mammals in the heat
of each other's moments and
when you are able to embrace
that moment

hold it tightly

let it not shimmer

from your hands

like mangled fairy glitter

but hold them closer than heart beats

let her be the one to control the breathing.

I found my voice in you.

It's weird how your opinion of a poet changes

when you are not sleeping with them.

When you sew what you reap
you have a nice, comfy blanket

Jesus
will have his revenge
in the meantime
would you care for a spot of tea
an endless, openless, misery
with a twist of lemon.

Oh yes Jesus will have his revenge
and even Mothra knows it
cause Godzillas are only made
for destruction.

Oh I like when other people judge other people
keeps the economy going
but you'll often find they are beating
the wrong dead horse
and Jesus knows this
        he senses it.

That's why they'll be no wrongful dead horse beating in this town

Oh yes
Jesus will have his revenge
with his spitfire-eye-things
and beams of light
and sparklees
and the hope honed
in everyone's eyes
as Jesus raises the dead
to replace the living

that's why I carry a shotgun and dictionary everywhere I go
just in case I ever encounter Jesus
just in case he just wants to test my vocabulary
just in case he wants to test the wraith of a desperate man
a loaded shotgun
and a plan
I looked Jesus straight in the eye
and he,
he turned away.

Why do some lovers just want to give a fuck?

Sometimes the only interesting thing about a lover
is how bored they make you feel.

"I want you to fuck me real hard in this gas station's bathroom."

I said, "You deserve better."
She didn't think so.
We did not fuck.
Maybe she thought I didn't deserve better.

I don't know what it is but lately all the lovers
I've become intimate within the past year
just want to fuck.

Not sure what's happening but I find myself
wanting to expose who I am
before exposing my penis.

Bliss is a tiger called ignorance
and the more lovers get to know me
the less they want to get to know me.

Maybe that's my fault.

Maybe I'm not the caring-giving-thoughtful man I thought I was.

Maybe that's all
I'm worth
just a fuck.

Sometimes the most interesting thing about a lover
is how alone they can make you feel.

Sometimes the best thing about a lover is when they leave

There are no regrets.

Not a single thorn.

Just a throng

of cradle cocoon kisses

sprout an ocean blue.

The clouds burst upon shorelines'
black graceful unsymmetry.

We waterfall dandelion thoughts
of afternoons in each other's arms

buzzing the birds into the bees

humming

a soft soul like breeze.

One of us will die one day

and one of us will become
an old jukebox song.

On my stoop

So I drink while I write and I write while I drink
to the light given off by the hum of the earth and
I try to focus on the details of the interaction
between the trees and people and how the
buildings respond to this and I drink and I try
to summon as much Ginsberg out of the leaves
that photosynthesis will allow and chlorophyll
is the best text to dream and breathe on while
smoking while trying to right that epic poem
I've been walking to sleep every night so you
see how I might get a little absent minded and
forget my dictionary on my stoop.

When I realized what I had done I raced straight away
to retrieve it but much to my dismay
my dictionary
had been murdered.

It was torn apart like a Neruda poem.

The only breath left is what heaven had to offer.

Why destroy a book?

Much more fun to throw it through
someone's window like a riot.

Side note: Children should not start riots until they start reading.

My palm aches sweat.
I pick up three quarters of a page.
It was the end of the *r*'s and the beginning of the *s*'s.

Those bastards.

Started reading some of the words and making up my own definitions.

rutty- *adj. in the fuck you sense-* like how grimy you got to be to rip up a dictionary.

ruthful- *v. or prayer-*my heart mourns the sorrow of pity and the patter of ideas.

My anger swells, then I see the word

Sabaism- *n.*- the worship of stars.

My heart swelled.

It took someone ripping apart my dictionary
to discover this beautiful word.

Someone thought to worship the stars and give it a sound.

Side note: Sounds are the notes of ideas hummed along with the music.

Someone thought to rip apart my dictionary

so I gave it a sound

a sunrise

a star.

Thank you

Abby Colman, Adrian Wyatt, Firefly, Aimee Herman, Amy Leigh Cutler, Advocate of Wordz, Bob Hart, Tom Bones, Brandon Perdomo, Brendan Wolff, Bryan Roessel, Cara Liander, Christina Fucaloro, Corrina Bain, David Lawton, Matthew Hupert, Eliel Lucero, Elliot D. Smith, Emily Keller, Enrico, Eric Alter, Erik Fucaloro, Erobos, Farah Fucaloro, George Wallace, Ian Khadan, Jaime Martin, Jane Ormerod, Jared Singer, Jeanann Verlee, Christopher "Jelly" Stanly, Jen Darci, Yeti, John Snyder, Jon Fox, Jon Sands, Jonathan Weiskopf, Kat Georges, Mark Bibbins, Kristopher Johnson, Lauren Williams, Lauryn Fucaloro, Dominic Iaenella, Lys Riganti, Megan Kellerman, Meghann Plunkett, Honeybee West, Mike Geffner, Nicole Fucaloro, Patricia Smith, Pete Darrell, Phoebe Blue, Puma Perl, Rachael Terres, Rod Morata, Rudolfo Leyton, Russ Green, Ryan Buynak, Ryan Moore, Thuli Zuma, Thomas Gibney, Todd Anderson, Vanessa Pele and to whomever fills my belly with radiance . . . you are all in here.

And thank you to my mom and dad for just being.

About the Author

Thomas Fucaloro is a NYC poet and editor for Great Weather for Media. His first book, *Inheriting Craziness is Like a Soft Halo of Light* was released on Three Rooms Press in 2010 to rave reviews. He has been on two National Slam Teams and is currently an MFA student in creative writing at the New School.

Books on Three Rooms Press

PHOTOGRAPHY-MEMOIR

Mike Watt
On & Off Bass

FICTION

Michael T. Fournier
Hidden Wheel

Janet Hamill
Tales from the Eternal Café

Eamon Loingsigh
Light of the Diddicoy

Richard Vetere
The Writers Afterlife

DADA

*Maintenant: Journal of
Contemporary Dada Art & Literature*
(Annual poetry/art journal, since 2003)

SHORT STORY ANTHOLOGY

Have a NYC: New York Short Stories
Annual Short Fiction Anthology

HUMOR

Peter Carlaftes
A Year on Facebook

PLAYS

Madeline Artenberg &
Karen Hildebrand
The Old In-and-Out

Peter Carlaftes
Triumph For Rent (3 Plays)
Teatrophy (3 More Plays)

Larry Myers
*Mary Anderson's Encore
Twitter Theater*

TRANSLATIONS

Patrizia Gattaceca
Isula d'Anima / Soul Island
(poems in Corsican with
English translations)

George Wallace
EOS: Abductor of Men
(American poems with Greek translations)

POETRY COLLECTIONS

Hala Alyan
*Atrium**

Peter Carlaftes
DrunkYard Dog
I Fold with the Hand I Was Dealt

Joie Cook
When Night Salutes the Dawn

Thomas Fucaloro
*Inheriting Craziness is Like
   a Soft Halo of Light*
It starts from the belly and blooms

Patrizia Gattaceca
Isula d'Anima / Soul Island

Kat Georges
*Our Lady of the Hunger
Punk Rock Journal*

Robert Gibbons
Close to the Tree

Karen Hildebrand
*One Foot Out the Door
Take a Shot at Love*

Matthew Hupert
Ism is a Retrovirus

David Lawton
Sharp Blue Stream

Jane LeCroy
Signature Play

Dominique Lowell
*Sit Yr Ass Down or You Ain't gettin
   no Burger King*

Jane Ormerod
*Recreational Vehicles on Fire
Welcome to the Museum of Cattle*

Lisa Panepinto
On This Borrowed Bike

Angelo Verga
Praise for What Remains

George Wallace
*Poppin' Johnny
EOS: Abductor of Men*

Three Rooms Press | New York, NY

Current Catalog: www.threeroomspress.com
Three Rooms Press Is Distributed by PGW

CPSIA information can be obtained at www.ICGtesting.com
Printed in the USA
LVOW12s1255080414

380524LV00004B/42/P